CHANGE PAIN TO GAIN

The Secrets of Turning Conflict into Opportunity

PATRICIA McGINNIS

INDIE BOOKS
INTERNATIONAL

ISBN-10: 1-941870-40-6
ISBN-13: 978-1-941870-40-2
LOC: 2015947902

Illustrations by Jon Steining
Edited by Sharron Stockhausen, stockink.com
Designed by Joni McPherson, mcphersongraphics.com

INDIE BOOKS INTERNATIONAL, LLC
2424 VISTA WAY, SUITE 316
OCEANSIDE, CA 92054
www.indiebooksintl.com

TABLE OF CONTENTS

FOREWORD

Conflict is one of the possible outcomes of diversity and differences.

We have the capacity to deal with conflicts effectively, rather than fearing them or trying to avoid them. As the title of Patricia McGinnis' excellent book expresses it, we can *Change Pain to Gain* through understanding and applying a set of "secrets" that help us turn conflict into opportunity. The secrets are specific skills we may recognize, but far too often do not fully understand or apply in conflict situations.

Using her extensive work as a trainer, teacher, mediator, and group facilitator, Ms. McGinnis discusses the practical secrets within a comprehensive philosophy of conflict and conflict resolution. In clear language and through the use of easily understood and attractive graphics, readers are empowered to become more effective in understanding and dealing with all types of conflicts.

Change Pain to Gain presents inspiring stories and real-life examples that enrich the secrets in ways readers can identify with and begin using immediately. Quotes from a diverse array of creative thinkers add further insight as well as humor.

Among many features of the book that impress me, two deserve special mention. One is the genuine and powerful way the author relates personal examples from her own life. It's as though she is having a comfortable, respectful, and enlightening conversation with each reader. The second feature is the creative and resource-rich Appendix. The Appendix in many books is often ignored by readers. Not in this book.

Readers will want to devour all of it.

Dudley Weeks, PhD
Author of the best-selling *The Eight Essential Steps to Conflict Resolution*

ACKNOWLEDGEMENTS

In my dispute resolution world, I see husbands and wives turn against each other, educators and parents spending tax dollars on adversarial conflict instead of on the education of children, and work teams feeling devalued by each other. There are ways to engage in conflict respectfully by intently listening, clearly communicating, and creatively solving problems. Please have an open mind as you read *Change Pain to Gain*. It may seem like the ideas in *Change Pain to Gain* are not secrets, but widely known ideas to many. However, this cannot be so. If the secrets disclosed were known already, there would not be so much conflict in our world that damages friends, families, colleagues, communities, and countries. I want you to discover, or rediscover, and use the secrets revealed in *Change Pain to Gain* to change your perspective about conflict.

I started engaging in conflict in a new way when my sister, Colleen Harris-Pearson, sparked my interest in mediation training. Her encouragement to enter the field of conflict resolution changed my life. I will be forever indebted to her for expanding my career and changing my life's path. She believed I had a natural capacity and personality to help others resolve conflict and I have enjoyed new windows of opportunity as a result.

One amazing opportunity I discovered was the apprenticeship program of the National Speakers' Association. Not only did the leaders expand my skills as a speaker and a trainer, they inspired me to write a book about my passion, resolving conflict amicably. One activity completed during the apprenticeship program was Meryl Runion's Brand Aid exercise which helped me crystallize my message in *Change Pain to Gain* and gave me the structure to organize it. I extend my appreciation to her and the Minnesota Chapter of the National Speakers' Association.

Finally, I thank my training colleague, Sparkie Ciriacy, who shared her training expertise with me and expanded my thinking about conflict. She has unique definitions attributed in the text, and she considered differences in personalities, conflict types, and normal group process as "imitators" of conflict. In our training business, Turning Point – Training, we use a new term, "masqueraders" of conflict.

SECRET 1

CONFLICT DOES NOT NEED TO BE FEARED

In great teams, conflict becomes productive. The free flow of conflicting ideas is critical for creative thinking, for discovering new solutions no one individual would have come to on his own.

~ PETER SENGE

Conflict. Fighting. Disagreements. Different labels create different feelings for people. Disagreement may seem less negative than conflict or fighting. But no matter what you call it, when people turn against each other, it's challenging.

You can meet that challenge by expanding your perception about conflict. When you open your mind to examine any conflict, rather than fear it, you learn more skills to help you address it. Sometimes you can even find humor in it. Enjoy some poignant and humorous quotes about conflict in Appendix A.

Secret 1

CONFLICT DOES NOT NEED TO BE FEARED

Conflict is a puzzle that typically creates anxiety. Does conflict need to be avoided, or is it a battle to be won at all costs? The answer depends on the situation. What is always true is that conflict is a natural part of life that occurs at the intersection of danger and opportunity. The best approach is to be neutral.

Many people think negatively about conflict and want to avoid it. Others want to exert their power and win arguments. There is another way to approach it, however. Think of conflict as an opportunity for creating better understanding between different people. Of course people have different ideas and opinions. It is normal human nature since people have varying lenses through which they view the world and any situation. The magnificence of life is found in the splendor of people's differences. Imagine an arboretum with only one flower, a symphony with only one note, or an advertising team with only one idea. No impact and not very interesting. It is the differences that bring beauty, music, and creativity. How people perceive and value differences in other people when they are in conflict will determine whether they have harmony in their lives.

Growing up in a family of nine presented plenty of opportunity for conflict as far back as I can remember. I am third oldest in a family of five girls and two boys, and we could claim the prize for sibling rivalry at its best. The middle child and my next younger sibling was Mary, my playmate and sometimes my nemesis. She was a cute little girl with blond ringlets and an angelic face. She had a speech delay, and I was often the only one that could understand her, so I was her interpreter. Our mother says Mary was the best baby of all. One early Saturday morning when we were playing house, Mary wanted the china doll my grandma gave me. When I wouldn't hand it over, she tried to grab it from me. I ran away, holding tight to my prized possession. As she was chasing me around and around the dining room table she would shriek, "Mommy, Patty won't let me bite her!" Her solution to conflict was to sink her teeth into it. It, of course, being me!

There may have been another way to handle this property rights issue. Had I considered the altercation an opportunity to practice conflict resolution, rather than conflict escalation, the scene might have played out differently. I could have just asked,

"Mary, what do you want to do with my doll?" I would have learned, by listening to her response, that she wanted to wrap it in a soft blanket and tuck it into a cozy cradle. While the doll took a quiet nap, she and I could go outside and have fun with our neighbor friends. That's what I discovered when our mediator mama intervened.

Better and more creative outcomes can be realized by simply considering conflict as the intersection of differences. I first heard of conflict being defined as the intersection of differences from my colleague and training partner, Adele Ciriacy, nicknamed Sparkie. She sees these differences intersecting in an adversarial or a non-adversarial way. Viewing conflict in this way has been invaluable to me from both a personal and a professional perspective.

> *Better and more creative outcomes can be realized by simply considering conflict as the intersection of differences.*

The Chinese symbol for conflict aptly demonstrates the intersection concept as it combines danger and opportunity in its definition. The Internet offers many Chinese symbols for conflict, but the one thing they share is the idea that conflict is the intersection of different concepts.

CONFLICT IS NEUTRAL

Are you willing to consider conflict as neither good nor bad? Seeing conflict as a natural part of life will allow you to change your mindset of danger, fear, and avoidance of conflict into a mindset of opportunity. Your new perspective will help you welcome differences as opportunities for creativity and problem solving. You'll be able to communicate more clearly, have better understanding, and enjoy improved relationships. Life improves when you manage conflict with civility and respect for the other person merely because that person is another human being. You can be a caring, empathetic person and resolve your differences at the same time. Imagine the possibilities.

People have different styles of conflict. Kenneth Thomas and Ralph Kilmann designed the Thomas-Kilmann Conflict Mode Instrument (TKI) in 1974 that shows there are five conflict styles. Some individuals want to keep the peace and accommodate the other person or figure out a way to compromise or collaborate. Others want to compete and win the argument, and still others want to avoid conflict.

What is your preferred conflict style? You, like most people, probably resort to what is most comfortable for you, but may not realize you actually need to use all five styles, depending on the situation. While situations change, no matter who you are, there is always the potential for serious discord.

Years ago I had a major conflict with Sparkie, my colleague I mentioned. The story we wrote about this altercation became our signature story (the story we were known for) as we trained groups in facilitating meetings and the resolution of conflict. It's an example of conflict that was not easy to resolve but worth the effort.

A TURNING POINT: GIVING CONFLICT
A SECOND CHANCE

Sparkie: Patricia and I like conflict; I assume you all feel that way, too, right? We actually know a lot about conflict. We are training partners and conflict is one of our topics. We suggest conflict can be a very good thing if it's seen as an alert to differences. If we are sensitive to the first small indications of conflict—the body language, voice, sense of discomfort—we're able to recognize it as the screaming message it is: there are differences here; take advantage of them! If we then stop, step back, become curious and look at those differences, analyzing what they mean and designing a way to use them productively, we can end up with some unanticipated and brilliant outcomes. The story of how we became training partners is a story about conflict that we would like to share with you.

Patricia: Sparkie and I discovered many differences as we designed a statewide training for educators in special education. For instance, I'm a big picture person.

Sparkie: I'm a bigger picture person.

Patricia: I also enjoy writing out the details of the plan.

Sparkie: Not me.

Patricia: I make to-do lists so I don't forget anything.

Sparkie: I lose them. I create visual cues, starting with pictures and graphics.

Patricia: I like words and outlines and notes.

Sparkie: I really like the process and discussing options.

Patricia: I want decisions and need a product. We can't talk forever; we need to start doing the training.

Sparkie: Okay, let's start.

Patricia: I don't know what my hurry was to start training. I was so nervous, with my knees shaking as I stood behind the lectern holding onto our script—every word of it. When it was Sparkie's turn, she roamed the room, responding to the trainees, not using the notes we'd developed. Interestingly enough, nothing terrible happened. I was intrigued. The next time we trained, I was a little more comfortable so I tried a more flexible approach, got creative, and didn't follow the script either. Very proud! After several trainings, Sparkie said she didn't like my creativity and went completely berserk.

Sparkie: Berserk is putting it mildly. Patricia was changing things during the training that had an impact on me. She'd say, publicly, "What about doing this activity a new way?" Again and again, I asked her not to say it. And she'd agree, then do it again anyway. I was so angry.

Patricia: I didn't get what her problem was. I thought I had stopped doing what she didn't like.

Sparkie: There came a time that almost broke us. During training, she asked me to do something new, and I said, "No." Immediately, I realized I looked like an idiot. I'd embarrassed myself, I'd reacted to conflict by ignoring its alert, and I'd done it publicly. I'll never do that again.

Patricia: I was angry with Sparkie, too. She had modeled flexibility and creativity, but when I tried to be these things, it wasn't OK with her. This was so unfair. It didn't look good for us, did it?

Sparkie: Once I stepped back from my anger, I got curious and began analyzing it. Was this partnership worth saving? Patricia was good at, and enjoyed doing, a lot of things I hated. Notes. Details. Lists. She could do those things, and I could do the things I liked. I realized the training—the product—was better with her than without her. However, we needed a new design —a new way— to allow our differences to interact in a way that would lead to a better product.

Patricia: I was analyzing what happened, too. This wasn't easy—to step back, analyze the conflict, and think about an intervention that would allow us to put our differences on the table in a way that felt safe for both of us.

Sparkie: We decided to meet once a week for breakfast, to listen "below the words," to summarize our decisions, and to give each other space to do what we each needed to do in our own way.

Patricia: The weekly intervention worked. I came to understand that Sparkie's reaction to me changing how we did an activity during our training, took her way out of her comfort zone. It was hard enough for her to remember the details of how to do the activities in the first place. Once we kept things on the table and listened more carefully, we were able to understand and to identify differences in each other that were valuable to the training.

Sparkie: As a result, we are using those very differences to create further quality trainings. We found our turning point.

Patricia: This is so exciting! If we recognize conflict as an alert, we don't have to be afraid of it, be defensive or get into a fighting mode; we can just stop, become curious, analyze what's really happening, and design an intervention that will make the outcome better than anything we anticipated. Would being able to do this make your world better, too? Why not try? Give conflict a second chance.

APPLYING THE STORY'S LESSON

If we couldn't work out a solution for ourselves, what good would we be in training others on how to resolve conflict? The depth of our commitment and the respect we had for each other's talents helped us reach a resolution and improve our working relationship. Whether man, woman, or child, conflict can be a challenge, but it doesn't have to turn people against each other. Think about the desired outcome and how you can reach it.

As a divorce mediator, I see couples no longer willing or able to resolve their differences. I'm saddened to see some people that had committed themselves to sharing their lives turn angry, hostile, and uncaring. I see my role as a mediator to bring civility and creativity to their process, however painful.

Conflict gives you the opportunity to determine what's appropriate in any given situation and whether your relationship with another person or achieving your goals is more important to you. Sometimes you give up one to have the other. In some situations, the best of all worlds is to have both through collaboration.

If you're like Winston Churchill, you will remember to see the humor in a situation or add some of your own. The story goes that he was having a heated argument with a woman who shouted at him, "If I were your wife, I would put poison in your coffee!"

Whereupon Winston answered, "And if I were your husband, I would drink it!"

Conflict is a natural part of life that occurs at the intersection of danger and opportunity—two differing concepts. Read on and discover how the next time you're faced with the challenge of conflict or disagreement, you can handle it with care.

SECRET 2

CONFLICT CAN TURN INTO OPPORTUNITY

How wonderful it is that nobody need wait a single moment before starting to improve the world.

~ ANNE FRANK

I envision a world where people engage in conflict because of their curiosity about differences. They communicate so clearly that they can see the world through each other's eyes. They understand and relish unique personalities and different styles of addressing conflict and tackling work projects. Work groups notice and accept their normal development. People design a world that respects individuals and communities. Diverse opinions not only survive, but thrive in this world. Creative solutions to relationship problems, education challenges, community efforts, and global strife abound. Nations resolve their differences using alternative dispute-resolution methods instead of bloodshed.

The first step in resolving conflict is being curious. Stop, step back, and notice the differences between your opinion and another's perspective. What emotion, if any, arises from your topic? If your topic evokes emotion, how strong is the emotion for each party? What life experiences or needs influence the other person's thoughts or actions? A very simple personal story illustrates this point. Being sensitive to design and space, I arrange our kitchen counter space appropriately (from my perspective), which involves placing the toaster in a specific place under the cabinet.

Each morning I discovered the toaster was moved, so I put it back. The next day, it was again moved, so I put it back again. After days of these repetitive actions, someone, namely my husband, got angry and banged the toaster into his preferred position, yelling, "Leave it closer to the window so I can see whether the toast is done!"

Secret 2

CONFLICT CAN TURN INTO OPPORTUNITY

The first step in resolving conflict is being curious. Conflict is often a riddle with a hidden answer that presents an opportunity for better understanding of another person's ideas that may be different from your own. It starts with your belief that opportunities for harmony and better outcomes can come from conflict resolution.

Neither one of us ever asked what the other person was thinking or why the placement of the toaster mattered. Had one of us taken the first step of curiosity, it could have prompted a simple question to find out why the position of the toaster mattered. Then, following the question with undivided listening would complete the process of understanding our differences.

Famous educator Carl Rogers once said, "Everything I've learned about others I've learned through listening." Once you've listened, communicate your thoughts and speak honestly and calmly, with integrity and courage.

Writer and teacher Dennis Rivers offers five dimensions of communication. Speaking clearly and concisely, using his five dimensions is critical for effective communication when trying to resolve conflict. The five dimensions Rivers suggests encourage you to focus on what you observed, how you felt, why you felt that way, what you want, and how what you want will benefit you and the other person. For example, remember those two siblings fighting over a doll in Secret 1? An easy solution would have been for the older sister to say, "Hey, little sister, when I saw you try to grab my china doll, I felt worried because I thought you were going to break it. Next time will you ask me first so I can share my doll without worry? We will have more fun together if we understand each other better." Of course our mediator mama may have needed to help us with this conversation.

> *...focus on what you observed, how you felt, why you felt that way, what you want, and how what you want will benefit you and the other person.*

Whether child or adult, conflict is an opportunity for better understanding of another person's ideas that may be different from your own. Having the courage to explore those differences rather than avoid them can improve and deepen relationships.

Conflict can produce either discord or understanding. You can avoid conflict, or you can engage with the important people in your life and explore the opportunities that conflict presents. How well can you let go of your perspective that conflict is always bad and needs to be avoided? If you are confident in your belief

> *You can avoid conflict, or you can engage with the important people in your life and explore the opportunities that conflict presents.*

that conflict is an opportunity and that you have the ability to give respect to others by listening, you can engage with people who have different ideas from yours, resolve many conflicts, and live in harmony. Try using the seven norms of collaboration found in Appendix B.

The next Secret helps you look at your current conflict reality so you can better work on creating your new reality that conflict is opportunity.

SECRET 3

BURNING ANGER JUST BURNS YOU

Internal conflict—Holding on to anger is like grasping a hot coal with the intent of throwing it at someone else; you are the one who gets burned.

~ BUDDHA

I n today's world, miscommunication, misunderstanding, and misinterpretation result in mistrust. People often think the worst of each other, call each other evil, and get angry, resentful, and retaliatory. They can be narrow-minded and believe their way is the only way to live life and solve problems. To them, everything is a competition instead of a collaboration. Unmet needs between friends, colleagues, family members, business associates, communities, and nations abound. Adults spin their wheels arguing about what is appropriate education for students while children lose out, miss out, and check out.

Rather than enjoying the possibilities of conflict, in the current conflict reality, people react in less than productive ways. Anger is one of those ways. Unfortunately, stomping out of the room, yelling, and slamming doors actually avoids or prolongs a conflict rather than shortening the angst many associate with conflict.

Secret 3

BURNING ANGER JUST BURNS YOU

It is no mystery that anger is not a productive strategy. Holding on to anger harms your body and your spirit. If anger prevents you from resolving conflict, it may result in a damaged relationship, isolation, loss of respect and trust, mood changes, even depression.

There are appropriate times to avoid conflict. One instance could be when you don't have time at that moment to address it. Another

There are appropriate times to avoid conflict.

instance could be when you don't have the information necessary that will bring the problems to light. Still another is when you are too upset and need time to think. These are all valid reasons and offering one of them in the midst of a disagreement is better than hiding behind unintentional anger. Use Appendix C to organize your thoughts so that when you are ready to address the conflict, you feel prepared. You hope the person that wants an immediate solution will consider your need to delay the discussion.

Without both parties showing respect for each other, the eventual conversation will become more difficult. Anger often breeds more anger, especially after someone slams out of a room when the other person wanted to talk. What might have been a calm discussion when both people were ready to share their perspectives and reach accord, instead can become a shouting match. Without respect, people get defensive. It's not pleasant to feel attacked and undervalued. When those feelings do arise, what's the typical emotional response? Anger, which leads to escalation of the conflict. People want their power back and will do whatever it takes to get it. In a family or between friends, the angry person may withhold affection, be passive-aggressive, act out by yelling louder, retaliating, or labeling the other as evil, uncaring, or stupid.

Recall the story of conflict between my colleague and me. When I became angry, it would have been easier to just say, "I need some time to think about this. Could we talk a little later this afternoon?" Instead of temporarily avoiding our conflict, we decided to continue our discussion and discovered a plethora of differences between us.

One difference—physical size—was even an issue. You may wonder why that should matter. Well, it did. Since she was a much taller and larger woman than I am, it seemed that she thought she could just roll over me and get her way. I felt threatened (notice emotions are involved) and was determined not to let that happen. I made valid contributions to the quality of the training, and I wanted my ideas used as part of the finished product.

We started into another disagreement about what we considered important content for the training, and I had had it! I was so angry I was shaking and could hardly control myself. Fortunately, we were in a public space that required self-control. It seemed like all we did was go round and round, without a solution. The poem in Appendix C captures the frustration of our never-ending cycle of bargaining. Had I suggested we finish our discussion about content at a later time, I could have avoided strong negative feelings towards my colleague. But instead of making the suggestion, I wanted to lash out, and as Buddha suggests, "throw the hot coal" as I held onto the anger and resentment for several days, even weeks. Unfortunately, I was the one getting burned.

The initial consequences of holding onto my anger were the autonomic responses of increased heart rate and upset stomach. Then came frustration and loss of respect for my colleague. I began to assume the worst about her. The inability to resolve the situation might have resulted in a damaged relationship, isolation, loss of respect and trust, mood changes, even depression.

We needed to focus our energy differently or risk derailing the project. Our thinking styles, problem-solving strategies, and project-management preferences were diametrically opposed. We had some major obstacles to overcome, and we needed to work together to find a way to overcome them. Keep reading to see how we did it.

SECRET 4

MY WAY OR THE HIGHWAY
IS THE WRONG WAY

Remember not only to say the right thing in the right place,
but far more difficult still, to leave unsaid the wrong thing
at the tempting moment.

~ BENJAMIN FRANKLIN

I was tempted to tell my colleague what I was thinking of her. It seemed overwhelming to address so many obstacles in trying to manage the situation and still realize our vision of facilitating an important training.

At times, it may seem impossible to continue in relationships with friends, or reach team goals with colleagues, if the people involved are close-minded, single-focused, shortsighted, disrespectful, or unwilling to take the time to listen.

In every facet of life, people experience obstacles to realizing their vision or feeling success in their relationships. At times, it may seem impossible to continue in relationships with friends, or reach team goals with colleagues, if the people involved are close-minded, single-focused, shortsighted, disrespectful, or unwilling to take the time to listen. Sometimes, we say the wrong thing or the hurtful thing.

Secret 4

MY WAY OR THE HIGHWAY IS THE WRONG WAY

Insisting on your way is the wrong way to go. No one person can be right every time. Maybe instead of my way or your way, there is another solution to the problem, yet to be discovered.

Every discussion with my colleague ended with her conviction that *she* was right and we must prepare our training according to *her* ideas. At one point, I was almost ready to give up working with her. The stress was too much. According to Maslow's Hierarchy of Needs, I needed to take care of myself.

American psychologist Abraham Maslow proposed his thinking in a paper called "A Theory of Human Motivation" in 1943. He suggested everyone has certain needs and there is an order to how these needs are met. Once the base needs are met, people move on to meeting the next level of needs. Once that level of needs is met, people concentrate on meeting the next level of needs, and so forth.

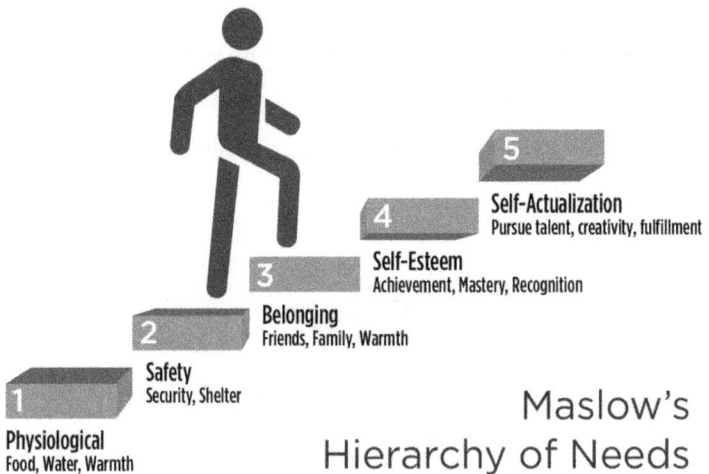

5 Self-Actualization
Pursue talent, creativity, fulfillment

4 Self-Esteem
Achievement, Mastery, Recognition

3 Belonging
Friends, Family, Warmth

2 Safety
Security, Shelter

1 Physiological
Food, Water, Warmth

Maslow's Hierarchy of Needs

Our issues weren't threatening my physiological needs, so first I needed to feel safe to express my views. Second, I needed to be accepted as part of the community my colleague and I formed. Finally, I needed recognition for my expertise.

Instead, I had a colleague convincing herself she was right and ignoring any data that may prove her wrong. A book written by Kathryn Schulz, entitled, *Being Wrong: Adventures in the Margin of Error*, quotes Benjamin Franklin who says it well, "I confess there are several parts of this Constitution which I do not at present approve, but I am not sure that I shall never approve them. For having lived long, I have experienced many instances of being obliged by better information, or fuller consideration, to change opinions even on important subjects, which I once thought right, but found to be otherwise." Kathryn Schulz suggests choosing words of doubt, such as, maybe, perhaps, hypothetically, debatable, occasionally, and conceivable when you are having a discussion or offering your ideas. In fact, if you read Schulz's book, after you've finished, you may wonder if you can possibly be right about anything!

It's especially difficult to manage situations when leaders, colleagues, or friends believe they are right and that their way must be followed. If they lack skills in communication, group facilitation, or conflict resolution to help manage relationships, meetings, and differences of opinion, other people lose trust in them and don't want to be around them.

Our economy requires people to do more with less, work faster, work harder, produce more and stay within budget. The pressure can be too much, so it becomes easier to be a bulldozer and run over people than to acknowledge others' thoughts have value. During those situations, people might use their power inappropriately. Unfortunately, then they are rewarded by getting their way. But at what cost do they get their way?

In the workplace—

>Employees may not feel respected when the management style is based on power *over* instead of power *with*. Using this style means those in command are not listening. When there are differences of opinion, these managers believe they are always right and know what is best, not only for the company but for the employee as well. The workers have no perception that the leaders care about employees as important contributors to the organization.

In homes—

>Whether in the role of spouse or parent, believing one always has to win every argument and being willing to use personal power to assure victory may result in damaged marriages and stunted emotional growth of children. One person can't possibly be right every time, yet a person thinking he or she is will become lonely, unsatisfied, and surrounded by unhappy people. No personal relationship can survive a self-righteous, uncaring attitude.

>*No personal relationship can survive a self-righteous, uncaring attitude.*

In schools—

>Administrators of districts and school buildings that see their roles as authoritarians will never succeed. If leaders won't listen when staff or parents

voice their concerns, teachers will quit and parents will open-enroll their children in neighboring districts. If leaders won't teach effective ways for children to resolve their differences without resorting to fighting, children won't feel safe. Discipline will be punitive, shaming, and ineffective. Likely, the focus would be on suspensions rather than restorative measures that teach alternative methods for resolving conflict and holding students accountable for the impact of their actions.

A decision to use your power is an important one. See Appendix D to reflect on your own use of power.

The next Secret covers how people can adopt valued principles for dealing with conflict when it arises.

SECRET 5

LET YOUR VALUES BE YOUR COMPASS

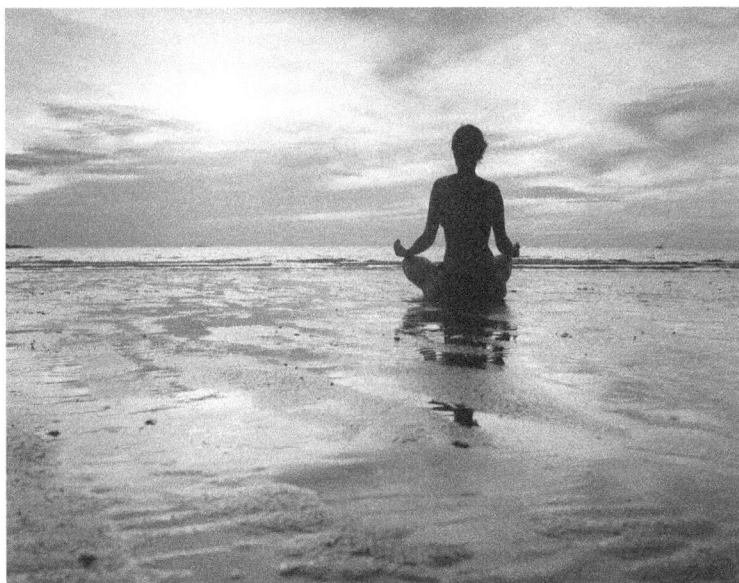

What lies behind us and what lies before us are tiny matters compared to what lies within us.

~ Ralph Waldo Emerson

Understand the principles that conflict is good, it is an opportunity, it is the intersection of differences, and it is necessary for better and more creative outcomes. Conflict is a fact of life and it will never go away, yet a calm, peaceful life is possible. People can be creative.

When in conflict, begin with the thought that people have gifts to be unwrapped. Operationalize that thought by giving people the respect they deserve and your undivided attention when they speak.

If these principles were shared among the members of families and communities, and the leaders in businesses and school districts, there would be relationships built on honesty and integrity. People would care, be empathetic, show respect, even in adversity, and be able to openly resolve their differences in a peaceful way.

Secret 5

LET YOUR VALUES BE YOUR COMPASS

Honesty. Integrity. Empathy. Your values are the clues to who you are and determine the choices you make. When you act consistently in accordance with your values, people will trust you. You will earn respect, and will inspire others.

When you value these principles as important, they can guide your decisions and actions as you interact with people and resolve differences. Your values shape who you are, determine the choices you make, and can influence an aspiration for creative conflict resolution. Values develop through the influence of friends, teachers, mentors, and community members, but first, they develop through your upbringing. Think about your beliefs and attitudes about conflict and how you respond when it occurs. Jot down your reflections in Appendix E. Both your immediate family and extended family have influence.

My uncle, the vice president of a major U.S. corporation and a man with undying integrity, was approached by his boss who told him to falsify an earnings report so it would be viewed more favorably by the stockholders. My uncle refused. When pressed further, he quit his job rather than act contrary to his values of honesty and integrity. This is a story told and retold by my parents to instill these values in my siblings and myself.

Similar to my uncle's values, my values affect the way I conduct business. For example, my care of others and desire to make peace guides my work as a mediation coordinator for school districts and parents of children with special needs. I listen without distraction when parents and school staff disclose their stories of conflict. The conflict is about the education of a child with special needs and the situation is intense and emotional for both parents and educators. They deserve attention and respect when requesting assistance to resolve a difficult situation.

Suppose I say I respect people, and then don't give them my undivided attention. Or, suppose educators say they care about children and then stymie a child's development because they are too busy to deliver the services the child needs. Consider parents who say they want their child to succeed, but then do nothing to support that child's learning. In each example, what message is being sent?

When values are not congruent with the words being said, people stop trusting and credibility is lost. But it is trust that is the foundation for strong relationships. Incongruency in actions defies one of the eight pillars of trust—character.

In professional speaker David Horsager's book, *The Trust Edge*, he defines the other pillars as consistency, clarity, compassion, contribution, competency, connection, and commitment. When people trust you, they can count on you. When you communicate clearly, you show you care about them, and they know you will act with integrity. If they need your help, they know you are capable and can get results. Finally, they want to be with you and know you will follow through on any commitment you make. Sometimes clarity in communication and congruency are difficult because of intense emotions.

Many years ago when my youngest sister Katie was dying, our family was in conflict. We argued about what was best for her, who should be with her and when, how to support our parents, and when to let her go, stopping all life-saving measures. Decisions started being made without consulting each other, which changed our mode of operation. This change produced serious conflict among our family members that led to more emotional pain at a time when we were raw with grief. We knew we were losing our nineteen-year-old baby sister.

Instead of letting the conflict tear us apart, we asked a neutral person, a counselor, to work through our differences with us. We could have walked away and decided resolution wasn't worth the effort. Instead, we recognized the need for apologies and realized the benefit and the healing that was possible with two words, "I'm

> *Instead of letting the conflict tear us apart, we asked a neutral person, a counselor, to work through our differences with us.*

sorry." As a result of working through our conflict, we renewed our trust and confidence in each other. We honestly shared our feelings and, as brothers and sisters, we acted with integrity and deepened our relationships.

Imagine what a problem-solving scenario looks like when you trust other people. First of all, you see people who care, who are open to others' ideas, and who respect each other. Acting consistently in accordance with your values will earn you respect not only from your family, but from friends, colleagues, supervisors, customers, and team members. Your values become your compass to help you consistently make the right decisions in collaboration

> *Your values become your compass to help you consistently make the right decisions in collaboration with others.*

with others. You inspire others to adopt your values. This is exact-ly what happened with my uncle's values of honesty and integrity and it's what can happen when you stay true to your values.

SECRET 6

STOP ASSUMING AND START ASKING QUESTIONS

Begin challenging your own assumptions. Your assumptions are your windows on the world. Scrub them off once in a while, or the light won't come in.

~ ALAN ALDA

I n managing a mediation program for parents and educators, I talk to people in conflict all day. What I notice is that people often assume and expect the worst and believe the other party will be unwilling to find a solution. So, sometimes an attack on "the other" begins.

Secret 6

STOP ASSUMING AND START ASKING QUESTIONS

Never assume, expect the worst, or believe the other party
will be unwilling to find a solution. Break the code by asking
carefully worded questions and carefully listening to the
answers as you imagine yourself in their shoes.

Once people stop making assumptions, conflicts can be resolved, sometimes without a formal process. For example, a parent who had a child with rheumatic fever requested mediation with the school district. While I was preparing him for the session, I heard his story. The doctor predicted the child would have to be home for at least three months in bed. The parent assumed the teachers and administrators did not care about his child because they did not offer to provide the student's services exactly how and when he wanted them provided in his home. In addition, the parent assumed the district staff were unwilling to resolve the situation. The district staff, on the other hand, assumed the parent had no medical or substantial reason for the demands he was making because he would not sign a release of information. They needed documentation of the illness before they provided such an expensive service.

The district agreed to provide homebound services after school hours and had a very willing teacher ready to begin. The teacher needed a schedule to accommodate her home life. She had a medically fragile child who needed to be taken to the doctor frequently after school. When I told the district that, similarly, the parent had medical appointments and lessons for the homebound child's siblings after school, which would be very difficult to reschedule, the district staff said, "Oh. I didn't realize that." And when the parent heard the district wanted to work things out, he said something similar to, "Oh, I didn't realize that." Working as an intermediary, we resolved the situation respecting both parties' schedules. It just took a few phone calls.

You may not always have a third party available to help you resolve your conflicts, but don't worry. You can work on resolution yourself. When encountering a difficult situation, ask questions. Be aware that the type of question matters. Your question should make the other person stop and think. Questions that begin with "what" or "if" or "how" will help you explore the situation and better understand what another per-

When encountering a difficult situation, ask questions. Be aware that the type of question matters. Your question should make the other person stop and think.

son needs to resolve the situation. For that to happen, you can't assume you understand the situation until you have asked for clarification. Be careful about causing the other person to feel defensive, which can easily happen by asking "why" questions. Instead, ask the type of questions I listed. Here are some examples to help you.

"WHAT" QUESTIONS

- What is important to you in resolving the problem?
- What is difficult for you in this situation?
- What matters most to you?
- What need will be satisfied if this problem is resolved?
- What factors, beliefs, principles need to be satisfied for a solution to be considered?
- What do you want me to understand the most about this problem?
- What are all the options we can think of to resolve this problem?
- What are the pros and cons of this solution?

"IF" QUESTIONS

- If this problem was resolved according to your wishes, how would that help you?
- If you could imagine the future with this problem resolved, what would it look like?

- If you looked back on this situation in five years, what do you hope you remember?

"HOW" QUESTIONS

- How will life change for you if this problem is resolved?
- How could we try out one of these solutions for a trial period?
- How will we evaluate whether the solution is working?
- How do you determine what is fair?

Once you ask the question, remember to listen. Then follow up with a deeper question related to the one just answered. I'm certain many have heard the well-known habit number five from Stephen Covey's book *7 Habits of Highly Effective People* that says, "Seek first to understand, then to be understood." It is by listening that a gift is opened. See Appendix F for a visual depiction and write down the questions from above that resonate with you. When you

> *It is by listening that a gift is opened.*

listen to the answers, you receive the gift of learning the other person's thinking process, how his or her perceptions have been influenced by personal life experiences, what is important to him or her, or what need he or she is trying to satisfy. By giving another person your focused attention as you listen, you show respect and your belief that he or she has something worthwhile to say. You show that you want to understand not only his or her words but also the underlying emotions, the motivation, personal story, and what influences his or her perspective. When you listen carefully, you can imagine yourself as that person, walking in his or her shoes.

Asking carefully worded questions can stop the negativity of assuming the worst of the other party because better understanding invalidates assumptions and illuminates reality.

By giving another person your focused attention as you listen, you show respect and your belief that he or she has something worthwhile to say.

SECRET 7

CONFLICT MASQUERADERS COULD DERAIL YOU

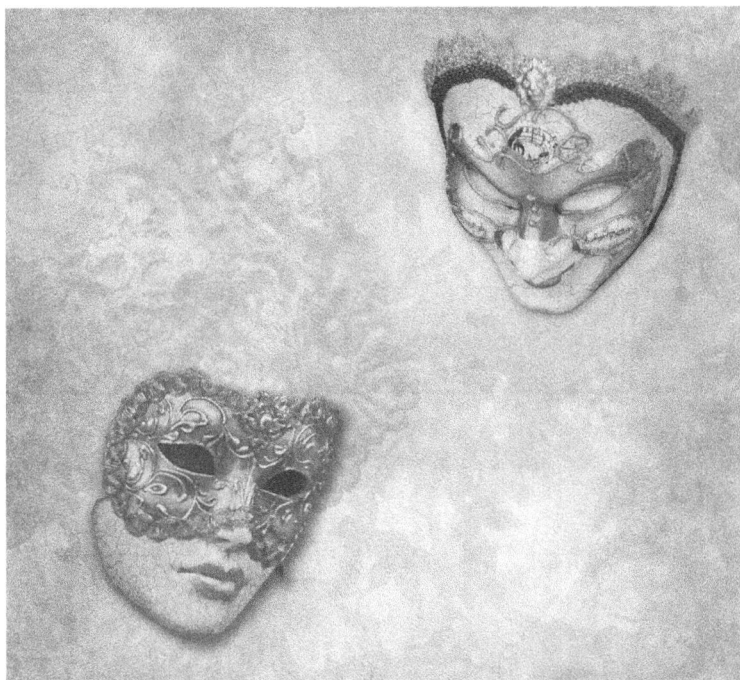

The real voyage of discovery consists of not in seeking new lands but in seeing with new eyes.

~ MARCEL PROUST

To create a more perfect world, some people need to refrain from assuming they know what others think and feel. Accusing others of ignorance, believing others have hurtful intentions, disrespecting others, and being biased that their way is the only way are thoughts that do little to promote harmonious living with others. People need to see the world with new eyes and know that conflict is an opportunity. Differences create more options and better outcomes. Some differences in people, however, masquerade as conflict. These differences aren't really the issue between people, but they appear to be, and get in the way of resolving true and substantive conflict.

Secret 7

CONFLICT MASQUERADERS COULD DERAIL YOU

Conflict can be inscrutable. Not everyone sees the world in the same way, and some differences in people masquerade as conflict. These differences aren't really the issue between people, but they can get you off track from resolving the true and substantive conflict.

CONFLICT STYLE MASQUERADER

One of those differences is personal conflict style. If yours is a secret to you, complete the questions in Appendix G to reveal your conflict style. Depending on your upbringing and your experiences, you may frequently choose one of five approaches defined by Thomas and Kilmann. You might remember reading about them in Secret 1.

One conflict style you may choose is to accommodate another person. You don't mind if the other person does something his or her way or makes the decision about what movie to watch, where to live, or what to have for dinner. The accommodating style is easy to use when the issues involved in the conflict are more important to another person than to you, and you want to preserve harmony and good will.

Another conflict style is avoidance. This style indicates the issue may not be important to you, you truly don't care, or you don't have time to discuss it at the moment. You may ask the other person to give you some time to think about the issue and schedule a time later to discuss it. On the other hand, you may think you will get your way if you avoid the discussion, so you walk out, slam doors, or leave meetings.

A third style is to compete, to win. Others may perceive your style as selfish, and think of you as a person espousing "my way or the highway." There are legitimate times to use this style, however. Specifically, use it when a quick decision is necessary to keep someone safe. It could be a principal requiring all teachers leave the premises for a fire drill or a parent demanding a child hold his or her hand when crossing the street. People sometimes use the broken-record strategy—repeating what they want in a non-adversarial way. While the competing style may get you what you want, it may also lead to resentment.

Familiar to many in negotiations is the personal conflict style of compromise, to split it down the middle and expect some give and take. While many think compromise is the preferred method of conflict resolution, it has some disadvantages. First, people may offer less support for the solution because they did not get everything they wanted, and the result is a win-some/lose-some situation.

Finally, and often encouraged for resolving many conflicts, is the use of collaboration to bring about a win/win outcome. If there is time to explore the needs of each party and there is willingness for creative problem solving, the outcome produces better solutions than the parties could work out on their own.

> *... often encouraged for resolving many conflicts, is the use of collaboration to bring about a win/win outcome. If there is time to explore the needs of each party and there is willingness for creative problem solving, the outcome produces better solutions than the parties could work out on their own.*

Your preferred style was likely influenced by your childhood. Maybe you had friends that accommodated each other so everyone could continue playing together, rather than getting angry and separating. You might have been part of a family that avoided conflict so the family members could keep the peace at all costs, or you could have watched one of your parents needing to win every argument. On the other hand, maybe your parents addressed conflict head on, figured out a compromise, and moved on. I was always amazed how my parents could have a loud, sometimes angry disagreement with each other, make a decision, and then hear my mom ask dad if he would like a cup of coffee. You may have experienced the fifth style in a classroom when teams collaborated as they worked on projects together and listened to each other so the end product was better than each classmate could have imagined on his or her own.

From our experiences each of us develops a preferred style of dealing with differences that becomes habit. The problem is our preferred style may not work in every situation, and conflict styles need to be appropriate for the situation.

The problem is our preferred style may not work in every situation, and conflict styles need to be appropriate for the situation.

In choosing which style is best suited to resolve conflict, it is helpful to look at the five styles according to the continuums of assertiveness/cooperation and relationship-building/achieving goals.

Think about a difficult situation that needs a solution, and determine whether you need to exert your authority and compete, or satisfy your interests partly (through compromise) or fully (through collaboration). If it's most important to be coop-

RELATIONSHIPS

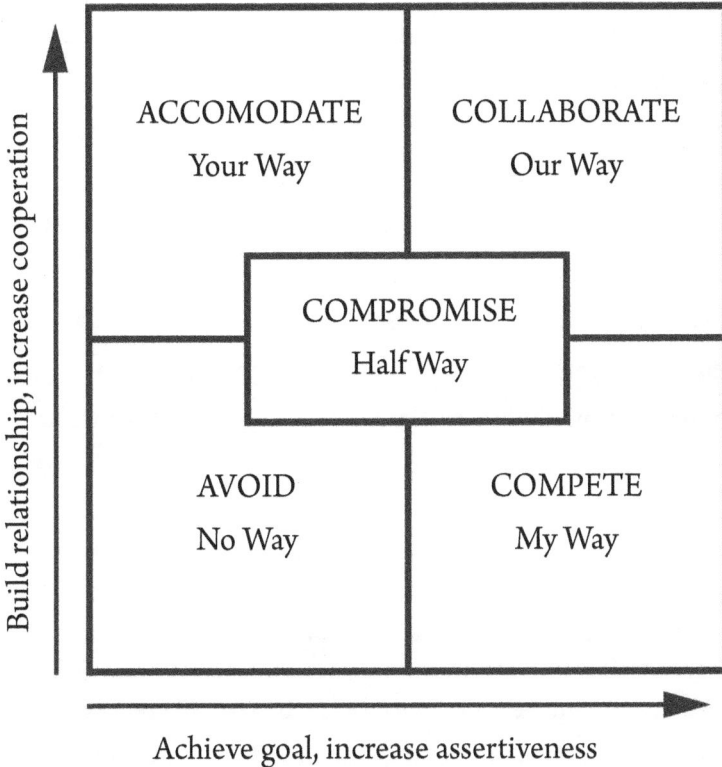

ACCOMODATE Your Way	COLLABORATE Our Way
COMPROMISE Half Way	
AVOID No Way	COMPETE My Way

Build relationship, increase cooperation

Achieve goal, increase assertiveness

erative and work together, then consider using the styles of compromise, accommodation, or collaboration. Ask yourself what is more important in each conflict – maintaining a good relationship or achieving your goal. There is only one style that addresses all four dimensions–collaboration. The four dimensions include:

- Being assertive
- Being cooperative
- Building relationships
- Achieving goals

Even with collaboration's benefits, it may not be the best style for every situation because it's necessary to consider several factors when in conflict. How important is the issue to you? How negotiable is the other person, and how much do you trust him or her? How much time do you have, and where are you? If you're in a grocery store or the hallway of a school, it may not be appropriate for resolving a conflict between parties such as a principal and a parent. Depending on the other person's level of hostility or anger, you may or may not be able to enter into a problem-solving discussion. If you're in a situation that requires immediate attention to safety and there is no time for discussion, one person has to win. In that case, use the compete style, and exert your power to keep people safe.

PERSONALITY DIFFERENCE MASQUERADER

Another masquerader of conflict is personality differences. The idea of personality differences was first introduced by Carl Jung in the 1920s. The work was expanded when Isabel Briggs Myers and her daughter Katharine Cook Briggs developed the Myers-Briggs Type Indicator (MBTI). The purpose of their work was to help people identify their personal preferences for various aspects of life.

According to Myers-Briggs, people are on four continuums ranging from introvert to extrovert, sensory to intuitive, thinking to feeling, and perceiving to judging.

An *introvert* gains energy from being alone while an extrovert is energized from being with people.

Another continuum describes how people take in information. One way is through senses by observing, using facts, analyzing data, and seeing details from which the big picture emerges. On the other end of that continuum is the *intuitive* person. The intuitive person looks for meaning and patterns while linking information and inventing solutions through inspiration and creativity. He or she sees the big picture from the start.

People are also different in how they make decisions. One person may be objective and use *thinking* or logic, wanting to weigh the evidence and get the facts. Another person may make decisions with *feeling*. They prefer to consider values, what's most important to self or others, and the impact of their decision on others.

The last continuum is about how people prefer to handle information and deal with the outer world. Some prefer making decisions or gathering more information. A *judging* attitude wants to do it right with a firm, quick decision. They want closure in order to reach settlement and move on. A *perceiving* attitude likes to take time, be flexible, keep options open, explore, and react to possibilities.

Two of these continuums come into play when we are in conflict and trying to resolve it—how we gather information and make decisions. When different types of people intersect during conflict, they often become frustrated, angry, and believe the conflict is insurmountable. Their frustration, however, may not be about the substantive conflict. They may be reacting to their different personality styles.

Listen carefully to the language used, and you can assist individuals in recognizing different personality needs and accommodating them. When a crisis occurs, you may hear, "I've analyzed the data and come up with an answer to fix the problem now!" This language offers you a clue the person is the thinking and judging type who gathered enough objective data to make a decision quickly.

You may hear someone else say, "Let's hear from each person on our team and take time to explore our options." This language comes from a person who is the feeling and perceiving type that focuses on values, a decision's impact on the people involved, and gathering more information.

So, what do you do if you are one of these people or you are assisting these people in resolving their conflict? You balance the process of the meeting with the outcome while addressing the needs of the people involved.

First, invite them to discuss their differences by creating a comfortable space in which to do so. That may mean finding a private space with comfortable chairs, providing light refreshments, and ensuring there are no distractions. You can check with the people in conflict by asking, "What would work for you?" so you are certain to meet their needs for comfortable space.

Next, seek clarity about the conflict. Both the thinking and feeling types' perspectives are necessary. Consider them equally to determine the focus of the conflict. Allowing parties to tell their stories and reflect their values adds meaning to the dialogue. Remember to validate both perspectives. Once the issue is clear, begin gathering facts that will accommodate the thinking type. Next, ask what is important to each party so the feeling type feels validated. Then explore several options to accommodate the perceiving type.

Finally, determine how parties will evaluate the options presented. If an agreement is reached on an option to resolve the conflict, be certain the agreement is written down so there is closure. While all parties want to be clear about the agreement reached, the judging type will especially appreciate this step. If there is no agreement, enumerate the next steps—agree to disagree, call in a mediator, take a break, try again, brainstorm new ideas, ask experts for assistance, or listen for other ideas suggested by the parties.

> *If an agreement is reached on an option to resolve the conflict, be certain the agreement is written down so there is closure.*

GROUP FORMATION MASQUERADER

When individuals come together as a problem-solving team, they may experience a third masquerader—conflict that is present naturally when a group forms. In 1965, Ohio State University Professor Bruce Tuckman published his theory of four stages to normal group development. In 1977, he added a fifth stage.

The first stage is called forming, and it is the time when people are polite, interactive, and act in socially acceptable ways. The second stage is called storming. This is when people start getting itchy, asking questions, perhaps getting aggressive, and trying out new ideas. They feel safe enough to consider conflict and no longer avoid differences of opinion. This stage may look like conflict. It isn't. It's as normal as a baby needing to walk before learning to run.

The outcome of productive storming is norming, the third stage. These are practices that become acceptable but aren't written down. A good norm may be that people don't interrupt each other, which is much better than a norm that develops where people are constantly involved in side conversations. Watch for unproductive norms and replace them with productive ones – curiosity, open-ended questions, listening to understand.

The fourth stage is performing. This is when people are productive, functioning well, collaborating, considering options, solving problems, and even having fun!

The four stages were joined with a fifth stage a few years later when Tuckman added adjourning. In the adjourning stage, the group dissolves after accomplishing its work.

Sometimes teams believe they are in trouble because members begin to offer diverse opinions or challenge each other. Once the normalcy of this pseudo-conflict is recognized, the group can accept it and continue to function and accomplish its goals.

Once conflict styles, personality differences, and group development are recognized for the masqueraders of conflict that they are, people can open themselves to explore the unique and valuable differences within their homes and workplaces and see conflict as an opportunity for better ideas and effective problem solving.

SECRET 8

EMBRACE CONFLICT TO FIND PEACE

One's mind, once stretched by a new idea, never regains its original dimensions.

~ OLIVER WENDELL HOLMES

Our world would be a different place if people would assume positive intent, if they would clear up misunderstandings by asking questions rather than deciding the other is evil, ignorant, or stubborn, and if every individual respected and accepted differences. The world would have less conflict if people could try to understand that another's opinion is just that, another's opinion. Of course, differences exist; the lenses people use to see the world are unique to each individual.

So, once again, how can people change the pain of conflict and damaged relationships into the gain of resolution and stronger relationships? Create a new normal by:

- anticipating differences rather than trying to prevent them;
- embracing the advantage of conflict—the intersection of differences—and producing better outcomes;
- knowing that personalities, conflict styles, and normal group development all masquerade as conflict;
- communicating clearly using the five steps;
- promoting collaboration when differences intersect;
- believing in the goodness of people and having hope in their ability to contribute to a group decision-making process;
- avoiding "divorce," the act of separating ourselves from others just because they don't think like us;
- having the courage to say what is difficult in such a way that it will be heard;
- seeking to understand.

Understanding another's perspective is crucial in many situations, especially co-parenting arrangements after a divorce. As a mediator, I assist parents who are fighting over their children before or after divorce, threatening termination of the other's parental rights, and pitting their children against the other parent. How does a child survive in such a sad environment? I am determined to influence the communication style of divorcing or divorced parents so the children not only survive, but thrive during their formative years. For example, I agreed to provide mediation for one particular couple who had been fighting for the ten years since their divorce. Years of frustration and anger in co-parenting after divorce were apparent when they began shouting at each other during the first moments of the mediation session, and the father threatened to walk out. Their angst was severe. No one was listening to anyone. Disrespect was obviously mutual between the parents. I had to raise my voice to be heard when I said, "STOP!"

Secret 8

EMBRACE CONFLICT TO FIND PEACE

Avoiding conflict can make matters worse. Resolve conflicts without running away, shouting at each other, or raising your blood pressure. Embrace conflict while you create solutions, protect relationships, and live in peace.

I followed this directive with a very quiet voice, which helped calm the parents and changed the dynamics. I persuaded them to do three things: (1) to listen to each other, (2) to give each other enough respect to allow them uninterrupted time to share their perspective, and (3) to retell what they heard each other say as well as how the other felt when the co-parent spoke. The result was powerful. Both parents felt heard, and they understood each other's perspective. As a result, their conflicts were resolved. Both parents not only thanked each other, the mother wanted to shake hands with the father, and he wanted a hug from the mother.

How can you use the eight Secrets you have seen with new eyes? Resolve the conflict without running away, shouting at each other, or raising your blood pressure. You have read ideas in this book that are offered to motivate you to a new practice. Your new practice can be summarized in three words: stop, sit, focus.

stop, sit, focus

STOP. Open your mind. Think about the differences presenting themselves and how those differences are intersecting. Use this knowledge as an alert to become curious and examine the assumptions you are making. Determine where the opportunity is in your situation and what outcome you desire.

SIT. Ask the person in conflict with you to meet one-on-one. Remember to ask open-ended questions. To fully understand, ask questions that reveal deeper thoughts rather than yes or no responses. Once you ask your questions, take the time to focus.

FOCUS. When the other speaks, listen. Listen below the words. Listen for the emotions. Listen to understand. Remember, listening doesn't mean you agree with what is said. It means you know how to show respect for someone else's opinion. It means you are capable of allowing someone else to feel heard and understood. Sometimes that is all that is needed to resolve a conflict.

Be confident in your belief that conflict is an opportunity and that you have the ability to give respect to others by listening with empathy. When you listen deeply you can better understand differences, resolve conflicts more easily, and live in harmony.

> *Be confident in your belief that conflict is an opportunity and that you have the ability to give respect to others by listening with empathy.*

In Secret 1, I told you about a fight over a doll that I had with my little sister, Mary. While sibling rivalry seems to be an unavoidable fact of childhood in many families, it doesn't need to be a fact of life as siblings mature. As my sister and I have matured, I have grown to have the greatest respect for her as a caring mother and grandmother, a talented artist, and an intelligent businesswoman. She is just plain fun to be with; I thoroughly enjoy our family and social events and look forward to more time with her when we retire from full-time work. Of course, we may have differences, and we will work them out amicably without holding grudges.

I mentioned conflicts I had with my colleague and training partner, Sparkie. After learning more about each other, appreciating each other's talents, and accepting our differences, she and I have collaborated on several training projects. We continue our conversations until we are communicating clearly, understanding each other, and resolving our own differences so we can teach others to do the same.

In Secret 3, I told you about a small difference my husband and I had about a toaster. At the writing of this book, we have been married many years, and I am convinced no conflict is bigger than we are.

As you go forward after reading this book, remember this simple definition of conflict. Conflict is an intersection of differences and an opportunity for increased understanding. Once you've examined different perspectives about conflict, taken time to listen and understand, spoken clearly about differences, and believed that conflict can be welcomed, the quality of your personal and professional relationships will strengthen. Deepen. Improve. You may even want to celebrate conflict at times. Imagine an approach to conflict that separates masqueraders of conflict from true conflict, and embraces a belief that every person can experience a significant turning point. It will change your life forever.

> *Imagine an approach to conflict that separates masqueraders of conflict from true conflict, and embraces a belief that every person can experience a significant turning point.*

If you recognize conflict as an alert, you don't have to be afraid of it or be defensive or go into a fighting mode. You can just stop, become curious, analyze what's really happening, and design an intervention that will make the outcome better than anything you anticipated. Use the worksheet in Appendix H to summarize some ideas that will remind you of what you want to think and do when you are in conflict. Then, make your world better by trying the ideas you learned in this book and giving conflict a second chance.

Now is the time to see the possibilities in using the secrets revealed to you and believing a new perspective is possible. Make this "moment of realization" your turning point from fearing conflict to embracing conflict while you create solutions, protect relationships, and find peace.

APPENDICES

APPENDIX A

Secret 1

CONFLICT DOES NOT NEED TO BE FEARED

Messages from Secret 1 are that communication may be difficult and that conflict is normal, even humorous sometimes.

An eye for an eye will only make the whole world blind.
~ Mahatma Gandhi

I'd agree with you but then we'd both be wrong.
~ Anonymous

The first step to effective listening is to stop talking!
~ Ken Fracaro

You can't shake hands with a clenched fist.
~ Indira Gandhi

Where all think alike, no one thinks very much.
~ Walter Lippmann

The direct use of force is such a poor solution to any problem. It is generally employed only by small children and large nations.
~ David Friedman

To avoid criticism, say nothing, do nothing, be nothing.
~ Aristotle

The rock, paper, and scissors say to each other, "Can't we all just get along?"
~ BrainlessTales.com

If you understood everything I said, you'd be me.
~ Miles Davis

Two angry people are fighting on Facebook. One says, "UhhhOh! She turned on the caps lock. This is getting serious now!"

I don't have an attitude problem, I just have a personality you can't handle!
~ Leave Me Alone Quotes and Sayings

My problem is I say what I'm thinking before I think what I'm saying.
~ Laurence J. Peter

APPENDIX B

Secret 2

CONFLICT CAN TURN INTO OPPORTUNITY

You will find conflict's opportunities by using these seven skills to collaborate with others.

SEVEN NORMS OF COLLABORATIVE WORK

PAUSING: Pausing actually slows down the "to and fro" of discussion. There are fewer "frames per second" to deal with. It provides for the precious "wait time" which has been shown to dramatically improve critical thinking. Pausing and the acceptance of moments of silence create a relaxed and yet purposeful atmosphere. Silence, however initially uncomfortable, can be an excellent indicator of productive collaboration. Pausing also signals to others that their ideas and comments are worth thinking about. It dignifies their contribution and implicitly encourages future participation. Pausing enhances discussion and greatly increases the quality of decision making.

PARAPHRASING: To paraphrase is to recast or translate into one's own words, to summarize or to provide an example of what has just been said. The paraphrase maintains the intention and the accurate meaning of what has just been said while using different words and phrases. The paraphrase helps members of a team hear and understand each other as they evaluate data and formulate decisions. Paraphrasing is also extremely effective when reducing group tension and individual anger. "The paraphrase is possibly the most powerful of all non-judgmental verbal responses because it communicates that 'I am attempting to understand you' and that says 'I value you' (Costa & Garmston, 1994, p. 49)."

PROBING FOR SPECIFICITY: Probing seeks to clarify something which is not yet fully understood. More information may be required or a term may need to be more fully defined. Clarifying questions can be either specific or open ended, depending upon the circumstances. Gentle probes increase the clarity and precision of a group's thinking and contribute to trust building because they communicate to group members that their ideas are worthy of exploration and consideration.

PUTTING FORWARD IDEAS: It takes a degree of self-confidence and courage to put forward an idea and it is vital that collaborative groups nurture such self-confidence and courage. Ideas are the heart of a meaningful discussion. Groups must be comfortable to process information by analyzing, comparing, predicting, applying, or drawing causal relationships.

PAYING ATTENTION TO SELF AND OTHERS: Collaborative work is facilitated when each team member is explicitly conscious of self and others—not only aware of what he or she is saying, but also how it is said and how others are responding to it. "Understanding how we create different perceptions allows us to accept others' points of view as simply different, not necessarily wrong. We come to understand that we should be curious about other people's impressions and understandings—not judgmental. The more we understand about how someone else processes information, the better we can communicate with them (Costa & Garmston, 1994, p. 59)."

PRESUMING POSITIVE INTENTIONS: Of all the seven norms of collaboration, this one may be the most fundamental, for without it, the rest are meaningless. Simply put, this is the assumption that other members of the team are acting from positive and constructive intentions (however much we may disagree with their ideas). Presuming positive presuppositions is not a passive state but needs to become a regular manifestation of one's verbal responses. The assumption of positive intentions permits the creation of such sophisticated concepts as a "loyal opposition" and it allows one member of a group to play "the devil's advocate." It builds trust, promotes healthy cognitive disagreement, and reduces the likelihood of misunderstanding an affective/emotional conflict.

PURSUING A BALANCE BETWEEN ADVOCACY AND INQUIRY: Both inquiry and advocacy are necessary components of collaborative work. Highly effective teams are aware of this and self-consciously attempt to balance them. Inquiry provides for greater understanding. Advocacy leads to decision making. One of the common mistakes that collaborative teams may make is to bring premature closure to problem identification (inquiry for understanding) and rush into problem resolution (advocacy for a specific remedy or solution). Maintaining a balance between advocating for a position and inquiring about the positions held by others further inculcates the ethos of a genuine learning community.

Like any new skill or behavior that has to be learned, these seven norms require practice and conscious attention. Individuals using them for the first time may find them awkward until the seven norms become more automatic behaviors.

Source: U.S. Department of State website

APPENDIX C

BURNING ANGER JUST BURNS YOU

Learn to name your emotions when you need to have a difficult conversation. Try this exercise from Dennis Rivers to prepare yourself.

1. When I saw/heard:
2. I felt:

   (Remember I felt that… or I felt like… is not naming the emotion.)

3. because:

   (why you feel as you do)

4. and now I want:
5. so that:

To get you started, here's an easy example that could have been used when my husband and I had a problem with the toaster.

1. When I saw *the toaster moved further under the counter again*
2. I felt *frustrated*

3. Because *it seemed that you were arbitrarily moving it and I didn't know why.*
4. Now I want *you to leave the toaster where I put it*
5. So that *I have enough light to see if my toast is done.*

This exercise could change the endless merry-go-round of conflict illuminated in Dr. Dudley Weeks' poem below.

BARGAINING

You and I, I and you,
seemingly trapped in an endless game
of merry-go-round
without the horses
of colors and fun, the music goes on
round and round

No harmony, no joyful refrain,
I pass you by, you knock me down,
you pass me by,
I knock you down,
we trade a few trinkets and make a deal
with painful sighs

But it's obvious that nothing's really changed,
for tomorrow's game returns to the same
round and round...
I want to get off before I lose

or find a savior to mend the wounds
on bloody ground

We've let ourselves entrap our minds
so we just keep fighting and making demands
as you try to give up
less than I do
and I try to concede less than you do
and act so tough

The leftovers after concessions are made
become the agreements we have to accept,
I've lost face
and so have you
and we'll grudgingly do what we have to do,
filling lost space

We both lie in wait until the next time
plotting the ways to exact revenge
pound for pound,
for concessions made
we're continually trapped in the same old game
going round and round

~ Dr. Dudley Weeks

APPENDIX D

Secret 4

MY WAY OR THE HIGHWAY IS THE WRONG WAY

Think about the relationships you have such as a significant other, spouse, friend, parent, child, colleague, supervisor, people you supervise, neighbor, committee member and decide for yourself...

1. In which relationship do you use your power most frequently?

2. In which relationship do you use your power less frequently?

3. When is it appropriate to use your power?

4. How can you use your power in a way that the other person accepts what you are saying and the relationship is not damaged?

5. When is it not appropriate to use your power?

APPENDIX E

Secret 5

LET YOUR VALUES BE YOUR COMPASS

THE CONFLICT CYCLE REFLECTION

Write Down Your Beliefs and Attitudes about
Conflict that You Developed as a Child

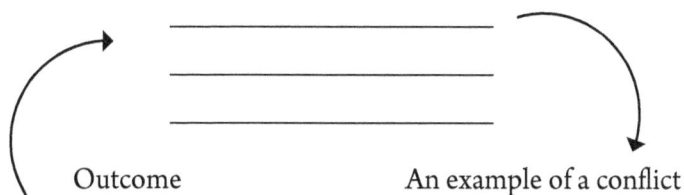

_____
_____
_____

Outcome   An example of a conflict

_____   _____
_____   _____
_____   _____

What I Do when Conflict Occurs

_____
_____
_____

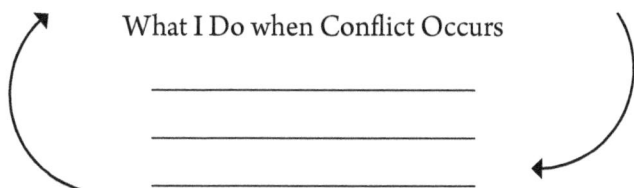

If the consequence of your response resolves the conflict, yet damages relationships, will you respond differently the next time? How do your values influence your response?

APPENDIX F

Secret 6

STOP ASSUMING AND START ASKING QUESTIONS

What questions will you use to open the gift of understanding another person's thoughts?

What...

How...

If...

APPENDIX G

CONFLICT MASQUERADERS COULD DERAIL YOU

SELF-TEST ON CONFLICT MANAGEMENT STYLES

The following test is designed to help you start thinking about your personal style(s) of dealing with conflicts. Please take the 10-15 minutes necessary to complete the test. It contains pairs of possible responses to conflict.

You will learn most about your own style if you think of a specific relationship (with child, spouse, work associate, etc.) as you choose the "A" or "B" response for each pair. Your choice will then be based on an experiential understanding of your tendencies. Because you may respond to conflict at work in a way that is very different from your response to a domestic conflict, you may want to take the test several times to discover your styles in different contexts.

In some pairs, neither "A" nor "B" may seem very appropriate; nevertheless, try to choose your more likely responses.

1. A. Differences are not always worth worrying about.
   B. I make an effort to get my way.
2. A. I try to find a compromise solution.
   B. I may sacrifice my own wishes for the wishes of another.
3. A. I try to win my position.
   B. Sometimes I let others take responsibility for solving the problem.
4. A. I try to do what is necessary to avoid tension.
   B. I seek other's help in working out a solution.
5. A. I give up some points in exchange for others.
   B. I assert my wishes.
6. A. I try to not hurt the other's feelings.
   B. I attempt to deal with all of her and my concerns.
7. A. I offer rewards so the other will comply with my wishes.
   B. I assume that in a conflict all parties may be able to come out winners.
8. A. I ask for more than I expect to get.
   B. If it makes him happy, I let him maintain his views.
9. A. I try to surface all her concerns.
   B. I sometimes avoid taking a position which would create controversy.
10. A. I propose a middle ground.
    B. I seek others' help in working out a solution.
11. A. I use whatever authority I have to convince the other of my position.

B. I try to find a fair combination of gains and losses for both of us.

12. A. I try to avoid creating unpleasantness.

    B. I try to soothe other's feelings and preserve the relationship.

13. A. In conflict, everybody comes out with something, though not all that was expected.

    B. I am concerned with satisfying all our wishes.

14. A. I don't let others abuse my rights.

    B. In a conflict, I may sacrifice my wishes for those of another.

15. A. I try to postpone the issue until I have time to think it over carefully.

    B. If it means more to the other, I let him maintain his position

16. A. I invite the other to join with me to deal with the differences between us.

    B. I assert my rights.

17. A. I will make an effort to go along with what the other wants.

    B. I attempt to get all concerns and issues out in the open.

18. A. Differences are not always worth worrying about.

    B. In a conflict, everyone should get part of what they want.

19. A. To keep peace, I will sacrifice my wishes for those of the other.

    B.   It's more important to be right than to be friendly.
20. A.   I try to do whatever is necessary to avoid tension.
    B.   I assume each of us must give up something for
         the good of whole.

Taken from: "Conflict Resolution Workshop" – Developed by:
Judicial Process Commission Conciliation Task force; Rochester,
NY (September, 1998).

Offered for use in the spirit of peacemaking.

SCORING
SELF-TEST ON CONFLICT MANAGEMENT STYLES

	Situations	Your Responses/Choices				
In each of the 20 situations, circle the letter you chose, "A" or "B." In the score column at the bottom of the chart, total the number of letters circled.	#1	A	B			
	#2			B		A
	#3	B	A			
	#4	A			B	
Then, note the name of the style in the column in which you had the highest number of circled choices.	#5		B			A
	#6			A	B	
	#7		A		B	
In the chart at the bottom of this column, write the name of the style (e.g., accommodate) in which you had the highest score and write that in the style column on the "1st" line. Write the number of responses in the "Score" column. Repeat that process for each of the styles.	#8			B		A
	#9		B	A		
	#10				B	A
	#11		A			B
	#12	A		B		
	#13				B	A
	#14		A	B		
	#15	A		B		

Order of Your Style Preferences			#16		B		A	
Choice	Style	Score	#17			A	B	
			#18	A				B
			#19		B	A		
			#20	A				B
			SCORES:					

To find out what conflict style your scores represent, please go to www.ChangePainToGain.com for an explanation and additional information about each style's advantages and disadvantages, the skills needed to use the style effectively, and the best time to use it.

APPENDIX H

Secret 8

EMBRACE CONFLICT TO FIND PEACE

Think about what alerts you that a conflict is brewing. Is it words, emotions, something else? Remind yourself of what you want to do next and your ideas of how you can find the opportunities in conflict.

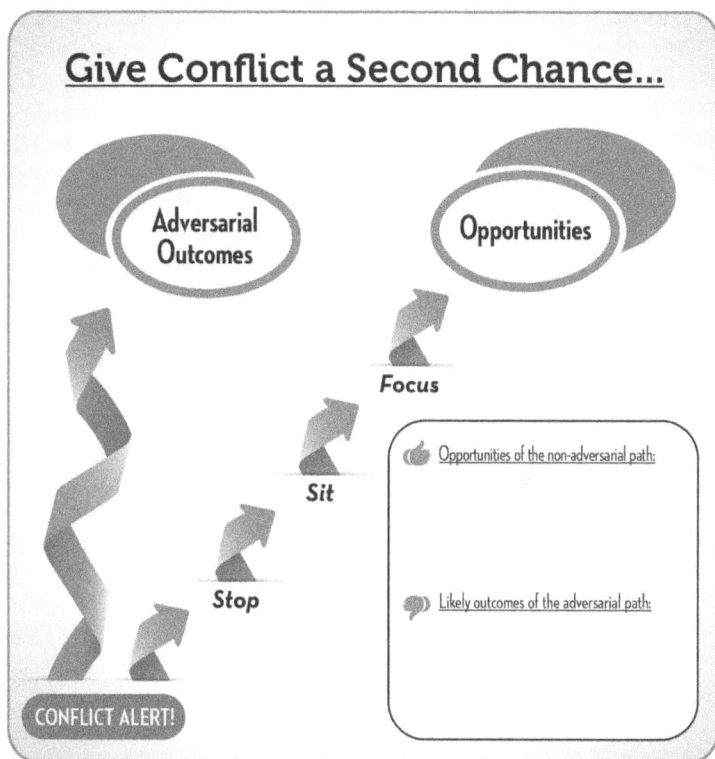

Give Conflict a Second Chance...

Adversarial Outcomes

Opportunities

Focus

Sit

Opportunities of the non-adversarial path:

Stop

Likely outcomes of the adversarial path:

CONFLICT ALERT!

ADDITIONAL RESOURCES

This is a list of websites and books that may be of use to you.

TEMPERAMENT:

- Keirsey, David and Marilyn Bates, *Please Understand Me: Character and Temperament Types,* 1984
- Killen, Damian and Danica Murphy, *Introduction to Type and Conflict,* 2003

CONFLICT STYLE:

http://web.mit.edu/collaboration/mainsite/modules/module1/1.11.5.html

GROUP DEVELOPMENT:

- **Bruce Tuckman:**

  http://www.chimaeraconsulting.com/tuckman.htm

  http://www.nsdc.org/library/publications/innovator/inn11-96hirsh.cfm

- **General Information:**
  http://www.scoutbase.org.uk/library/hqdocs/facts/pdfs/
  fs140042.pdf

  http://www.teambuildinginc.com/tps/020b.htm

CONFLICT RESOLUTION:

- Weeks, Dudley, *The Eight Essential Steps to Conflict Resolution*, 1994

- Socratic Questioning, http://ed.fnal.gov/trc/tutorial/taxonomy.html

- Cloke, Kenneth & Joan Goldsmith, *Resolving Conflicts at Work: A Complete Guide for Everyone*, 2001

- Fisher, Roger and William Ury, *Getting to Yes: Negotiating Agreement without Giving In*, 2011

- Ury, William, *Getting Past No: Negotiating with Difficult People*, 1993

- LeBaron, Michelle, *Bridging Cultural Conflicts: A New Approach to Changing the World*, 2003; *Bridging Troubled Waters: Conflict Resolution from the Heart*, 2002

- Mayer, Bernard, *The Dynamics of Conflict Resolution: A Practitioner's Guide*, 2012

ABOUT THE AUTHOR

Patricia McGinnis' work is about disagreements. Addressing conflict, rather than avoiding it, has always been her approach to interpersonal relationships. In her early years as a parent, she dealt with two quarreling children by having them sit in two chairs across from each other. With her assistance, they kept talking until they worked out a solution to their problem. Through articles she wrote as a coordinator of an Early Childhood Family Education program, she taught parents how to address sibling rivalry and make peace in the family.

McGinnis earned an education degree from the University of Minnesota and has many years of teaching experience. In her position as coordinator of the Minnesota Department of Education Special Education Alternative Dispute Resolution Services, she prepares parents and educators to resolve their conflicts over the education of students. Through Turning Point-Training, she and her colleague teach communication, facilitation, and conflict resolution skills across the country for administrators, work teams, and special education leaders.

McGinnis is a group facilitator, a coach for professionals who facilitate difficult meetings, and has taught Conflict Management for Administrators at the university level. She is a qualified neutral on the Minnesota Supreme Court Rule 114 Roster and mediates divorce and post-divorce conflict.

McGinnis lives with her family in the Twin Cities area of Minnesota.

PATRICIA MCGINNIS

Turning Point – Training

Patricia McGinnis is a speaker ready to talk with your group on how to use the Secrets to communicate clearly, and embrace conflict to find peace. She will work closely with you to deliver what your people need and want.

To inquire about booking Patricia as a speaker, or for more information on discounted bulk sales of this book, please send her an e-mail at patricia@tp-t.com.

Patricia and her training partner, Sparkie Ciriacy, offer presentations and training on communicating effectively, resolving conflict creatively, and facilitating difficult meetings successfully. Often referred to as the "Dynamic Duo," they inspire people to work together better. They provide information and tools that support the learning process, and motivate people to put ideas into action.

Visit our website or send an e-mail for more information. We'd love to hear from you!

www.tp-t.com

patricia@tp-t.com